LESSONS LEARNED

RUBY SIMMONS

Lessons Learned
Copyright © 2025 by Ruby Simmons.
Cover image, courtesy of Honey Pot Performance: Ladies Ring Shout 2.0

All rights reserved. No part of this publication may be reproduced, distributed, or transmitted in any form or by any means, including photocopying, recording, or other electronic or mechanical methods, without the written consent of the publisher. The only exceptions are for brief quotations included in critical reviews and other noncommercial uses permitted by copyright law.

MILTON & HUGO L.L.C.
4407 Park Ave., Suite 5
Union City, NJ 07087, USA

Website: *www. miltonandhugo.com*
Hotline: *1- 888-778-0033*
Email: *info@miltonandhugo.com*

Ordering Information:
Quantity sales. Special discounts are granted to corporations, associations, and other organizations. For more information on these discounts, please reach out to the publisher using the contact information provided above.

Library of Congress Control Number:		2025912345
ISBN-13:	979-8-89285-583-9	[Paperback Edition]
	979-8-89285-584-6	[Digital Edition]

Rev. date: 10/02/2025

CONTENTS

Dedication vii
Prologue ix
The Scout Ship 1
About the Author 3
1 The Friendship 5
2 The Flagship 15
3 The Situation-Ship 33
4 The Captain of *My* Ship 45
Borrowed Quotes and Images 59

DEDICATION

This book is dedicated to past lovers FROM whom I have learned so much about myself. Thank you for the time we shared and the timing of the lesson.

PROLOGUE

This poetry book is a compilation of different poems and a few short stories about past loves and experiences that I have had, and the lessons that I have learned either through heartbreak or the energies simply dissipating.

They say that people come into our lives for either a reason/a lesson, a season, or a lifetime. Part of what I've learned is that this is not always made immediately clear. We have to spend time, become intimate, or simply talk until all subjects and interests have been exhausted to gain a clearer picture of the other person's intentions toward you. On the other hand, some show you right away who they are and what they are there for, and we don't always listen; we hang around hoping it's not true, or thinking that we can change them, because "we are so special, and can love them better". Boy, was I naive!

In re-reading my poetry journals and scrapbooks, I discovered how much I have grown since my last serious relationship and my most recent 'situation-ship'. It inspired me to put them all together for public consumption and not worry if I get judged, but rather hope that it gives some other soul some sense of solidarity in healing.

THE SCOUT SHIP

"I'M 22, BUT I'M STILL A KID"

Like Dorothy dipping her toe in the pool, I took a dive and tried my hand at being in love...

Untitled

Baby, baby...When we first met, I never felt anything so strong. You were like my lover and my best friend, all wrapped into one with a ribbon on it. And all of a sudden, you went left...

———

Damn! Ain't it funny when you're listless, you'd do anything to feel again, feel him, again...?

ABOUT THE AUTHOR

Ruby Simmons ~ multi-dimensional Haitian American artist who pursued her secondary education in writing and journalism. Growing up, her parents exposed her to black poets, classic poets, and many different literary geniuses of diverse backgrounds. While also ensuring that her musical background was just as diverse, they played songs for her from an array of different genres. When they didn't have the words to comfort her from heartbreak, they would play songs to better articulate how to overcome that hurdle. This greatly influenced her writing style and ongoing passion for creative writing.

When it came to love, her parents taught her to "be the high fruit." Initially, that was a foreign concept. However, through her journey to find love, she has come to understand EXACTLY what they meant! Now, she's passing that lesson on to her child: "Be the high fruit." In other words, strive to be your best self, not so easily accessible or attainable by others.

THE FRIENDSHIP

"YEAH, WE CAN BE FRIENDS."

Just a Chi-Town girl, runnin' 'round this crazy world, she took the midnight 'L' going anywhere...

Sweet Kiss

Take some soap… wash the face.
Take some toothpaste… brush the teeth.
Take a towel… dry the face, dry the mouth.
Pick out some Chapstick… smooth the lips.
Take the gloss… shine the lips.
Find your love… kiss their lips, their mouth, their face.
Love them up in your sweet kiss.

Rainy Day (2009)

Today is a rainy day, it's cold.
I miss family.
I miss friends.
I miss my room, I miss my window.
Today is a rainy day, it's cold.
The sky, uninviting,
The sun has gone to bed with a cold.
God is crying for the sick and unhappy.
Today is a rainy day. It's cold.

For the Loveless (2009)

For the loveless, I pray.
I pray they *find* happiness instead.
For the loveless, I pray.
I pray they *want* happiness instead.
For the loveless, I pray.
I pray they *need* happiness instead.
For the loveless, I pray.

"Ill-legit" (lyrics from 2005)

"Oh, I can't wait to get home. I've been gone too long. Ooo, I just wanna lay with him, feel his body against mine. I wonder if he knows that I can't get him off my mind…I love him, I do…"

Been away for a while, but came home to you.

Couldn't wait for your smile and all the sexy things you do.

I was sittin' in my tub…Wishin' I could feel you rub, on my body, fill me up with your love.

Thinkin' bout those nights I was cold'n alone, then you hit me on the cell to let me know you're at home.

Your touch…

Drives me wild, kiss that makes me go ahhh between my thighs.

Oh my God! You got my body achin', put it on me baby, always got my bed quakin'.

Make it last, got me shakin', vibratin', and forgettin' my past.

In My Yard Today...

In my yard today… I sit at first, but my toes are too excited to be still. My toes, freshly painted, guided my feet eagerly into the cool moistness of the lawn. I run up and down the length of the grass, back and forth, flinging my arms open wide, as if to invite the warm breeze in for a big hug.

Finally, I sit, plopping down in the sun. I close my eyes, tilt my head back, and listen. Listen to the birds talk to each other, listen to the squirrels dig up and eat their nuts, listen to the wind play the chimes on the house next door. And then, at last, I listen to the wind Himself.

Listening, my eyes still closed, and the sun warming my face, I hear Brother Wind tell me to "remember, remember, remember." Slowly, I see darkness, I feel the ground trembling beneath my aqua green toes, and my body feels in motion, as if on a roller coaster. Slowly, the speed of my journey picks up, faster, and faster, and faster; spinning me, twirling me, changing me, throwing me, shaking me, and a bright orange warm light!

It fills me with warm, jovial feelings. Feelings I haven't felt in a year. I hear Brother Wind whisper in an 'oh so gentle' voice, still booming, say, "Open your eyes!"

Spoken From My Heart!

I sit and think of all of our moments together…

It brings about a reminiscence of our blossoming that has been ongoing. I've realized how much I need you; however, hard it is to say out loud, it's true, it's oh so true!

Not in a desperate, dependent way, but like a cactus sustains itself until the rain comes, or until the gardener tends to it.

Always growing, living, and blossoming on its own. But like my desert friend, I need you to, once in a while, tend to me like the rain or the faithful gardener, as I am willing to tend to you.

Water my soil, reassure me that things are "okay", balanced, good… And I will reciprocate this affection.

Like this little green mystery that we are akin to, somehow, we're able to go long periods alone, reflecting, rearranging, growing, expanding, and just being.

You need to know that I can stand on my own two feet, like I know you can, but I'd rather stand by your side than have you carry me, although I am willing to carry you. Let's hold each other up in equal strength.

"Tek"...My Twin Flame (2005)

Your eyes...

Like two dark marbles drifting over the curves of my slender body, making my skin glow with warmth, you lean in to kiss me with lips as soft as silk...

My body...

Melts into yours, my mind spins into a dizzying whirlwind of beautiful gold and papaya orange hues.

I open my eyes and look deep inside you and see my future, our future. I see us growing and changing as we mature.

To feel your hot, smooth skin pressed fervently against mine. You hold me tight, showing me the strength of a warrior... ancestral strength.

Your body is like artwork! Making me want to run my fingers over the smooth, velvety, fine details of your chiseled features as if carved from sunstone.

Early in the morning, as we collapse beside each other, soaking up the warm rays of the sun, your body heaving and sweaty reminds me of the Pharos loved by my body, glowing and moist, your ever faithful Queen.

Patience

Beep! Beep! Beep!

My alarm, rushing me awake and into my day. Slowly, I get out of bed, and the race starts. Rush to the bathroom, quick shower, air dry. Wonder what he's doing today… If I'm on his mind too. No scented lotion, no perfumes, nothing sweet about this morning…

Ring! Ring! Ring!

My phone, rushing me out the door, on my way into the world. Slowly, I ease into my car, and the countdown for the Indy 500 plays in my head. Get to the store, people rushing, pushing, bustling, racing through life. Drop my carton of eggs. Oh, what I'd give to hear his soothing voice right now, don't do it… Ruby, don't be thirsty, don't call! Nothing cool about the grocery store…

Tic toc! Tic toc! Tic Toc!

Life is rushing by like a clock. Time to find someone to love, build a family, leave a legacy, finish school, start your career! Too many heartbreaks, heartaches, and headaches. The pressure to perform, to deliver, to produce, to reproduce. I miss him dammit! Why can't I be the first to call? Nothing right about expectations…

In need of a break, a reset, a space to feel… anything other than the day-to-day flood of reality… I'm gonna do it, I'm gonna call him! Slowly I pick up the phone and dial 3-1-2… hesitation setting in, 9-0-9… doubt taking over, 1-3-6… "Oh, Ruby, just do it!"…2

Ring! Ring! Ring!

"Hello!"

"Hi!"

Patience *is* a virtue.

THE FLAGSHIP

"HERE WE GO!"

AS IF A SWIRLY, TWIRLY DERVISH...

Untitled (2007)

Baby, baby...

    When we first met, I never felt anything so strong. You were like my lover and my best friend, all wrapped into one with a ribbon on it. And all of a sudden, you went left. I didn't know how to follow; it was like the shock had spun me 'round, and now my heart felt empty and hollow. I'll never give myself to another the way I gave it to you. You don't even recognize the ways you're getting to me. It's gonna take a miracle to bring me back, and you're the one to blame.
    And now, I feel like oooh, you're the reason why I'm thinking, 'I don't want to smoke these cigarettes anymore" I guess that's what I get for wishful thinking. I should've never entered your door. Next time you want to leave, I should just let you get out and go, 'cuz now I'm smoking like I bleed. Might need to check into rehab, 'cuz baby, you're my disease.
    Damn! Ain't it funny when you're listless, you'd do anything to feel again, feel him, again...? Anytime you needed me, I'd be there, like you were my favorite drug.
    The only problem was that you were using me differently than I was using you. But now that I know it's not meant to be, I gotta go, gotta wean myself off of you.

I Cry (2007)

Ohh! Ow!
Ow! Oh!
My heart screams out.
My soul broken and beat.
Beat with sorrow.
Beat with pain.
Beat with depression and madness.
Loving you is like being in the ring with Tyson.

Some Things

Some things in life are worth the wait...
Some things in life are worth a fight...
Some things in life are worth your time...
Some things in life are worth your dime.

Wondering

I wonder, sometimes, if people enjoy a free smile or a hug...

I wonder, sometimes, if people appreciate a gentle caress or a soft kiss...

I wonder, sometimes, if people like being told how beautiful or handsome they are...

I wonder, sometimes, if people know that someone loves them...

I wonder...

A Letter

Dearest,

You take my breath away. From the moment I met you, your smile has brightened every day. Your eyes were the first thing that caught my attention. The deep brown of them captured me. They were so warm, intriguing, and inviting. The chemistry I feel between us is electric. You have invaded my thoughts and senses... and I like it.

The truth is, I have never met anyone who makes me smile as much as you do. You make me feel like singing, cooking, dancing, writing, and painting. In the short time that I have known you, I have honestly been happier than I ever have before.

I want to be the reason that you smile, the reason why you dream. I want to be your woman, your peace, and make you proud to be my man.

Always,
Ruby

Untitled (2005)

You blasted into my life and made me feel this shit was right...
Every night, gettin' it on and can't stop til 6 in the mornin'.
Got me steamin', feenin', and screamin' your name...
If you left me now, you know I would fo' sho go insane.
At Lover's Lane, wearing pretty panties for you...
And when you give me that look, I know just what to do.
Baby, we go together like milk and honey...
Your sweet love holdin' me down, never about the money.
Without it, my love, you know I'll still be around.

Planet Chocolate (2022)

Already comfortable putting your hands on my skin.
Hugging me tight like we're already family.
The way you looked at me with familiarity…
I realized I already knew you. Your scent, your swag, your sound; drew me in like flies to honey… irresistible.
Your chocolate skin, so smooth and shiny. Your smile, all white and gapped so perfectly, made me smile.
When you asked me to dance with such cool confidence, it made me feel wanted.
You were so sure with every move you made in my direction; it made me sure…
Sure, I wanted to know more.

The Perfect Thing...? (2022)

The perfect thing, I never thought of...

Your smile, skin, eyes... all pleasant surprises from across the room.

I fought hard against your charm, knowing that my interest was piqued.

You knew what you wanted and never faltered... like water on the jagged rocks, you crashed over me.

I enjoyed the challenge of trying to resist *you* and watching you blush.

Speaking with you was interesting, intriguing, and exciting. Mad at myself for not being open to you sooner...

Not sure what opened my eyes to you and the truth about how you feel and what you knew after the first time you saw me, but I have eyes wide open; I see you, and I love the view.

...Time is a funny thing.

MiTBoNa

Tall, handsome, silly, brown skin, and pearly white teeth.

Completely unattainable, romantically and emotionally, yet somehow still mine...

Sexy, sensual, wild-hearted, and complex.

Deep thinking, go-getting, never settling for less... or settling at all.

Finding myself enamored and head over heels with no place to land... floating.

We share an incredible connection, real fun, easy conversation, deep exchanges, and serious physicality.

Every moment between us lingers around me like incense smoke... sweet, filling the air with romantic ancient swirls.

Mi, T, Bo, Na...

Still In My Yard Today…

I open my eyes to find myself in my dorm room on the first night after moving in. I'm playing cards with Angie, Liz, and Jonathan. I turn to a mirror and look at my face to see such innocence, such light, and so much life. I hear my laughter, crisp, clear, and happy. It gives me goosebumps to see that… In a flash, my chair is on the move again…

Zipping through the space in my head, the chair comes to an abrupt halt, and Brother Wind tells me, "Breathe deep, Black Girl." With these instructions in hand, I take a breath really deep and long. The air is familiar, and as I look around, the scene changes, and I'm riding down Lake Shore Drive with Sal. On a beautiful Chicago Spring morning, hanging out with him was always fun. I was always myself, free to be silly, be nerdy, be sexy, be me. A version of myself that I miss, but am glad to know there is the memory of.

Whoosh! My chair is moving through the galaxy of memory again, and this stop on the ride takes me to a place close to my heart: 44th and Drexel… Oh! Oh! The memories!

Reverberations

Ripples and waves from the way you touch me. Your hands move over my skin, gliding, grasping, gripping... spanking.

Slippery wet at the thought of you, and well after we finish. I smile to myself at random moments, remembering every sound, taste, thrust, and kiss.

I see your smile when I close my eyes. I feel your skin on mine when the wind blows softly across my cheek.

Your mouth tastes like chocolate, whiskey, and backwoods. Sweet and smoky. Your tongue wet and thick exploring my mouth and other places; sucking, nibbling, licking, kissing.

Slowly, you land your spaceship, deeply thrusting, rocking gently, increasing your tempo until I'm screaming your name.

That sexy way you ask, "There?"

"YES! RIGHT! THERE!"

You celebrate the moist, tight, warm space of my portal, as I luxuriate in how strong your rhythm is, the strength in your stroke... harmonic convergence.

As vibrant as our undressing sessions are, I crave a chance to return the favor. I want to taste you, rub you, ride you the way you prefer. Watch your eyes glow with pleasure and reciprocate the ripples and waves.

Mr. G

Oh wow,

When I think of you, there is so much that happens. Music plays, my skin tingles, my heart smiles, my brain is intrigued. I find myself wondering what you're wondering. I want to know everything about you. I want to share everything with you. You evoke this insatiable curiosity in me, making me feel intimidated *and* insecure; I can't understand it. Your magnetism is addictive. You are so cool, intelligent, chill, familiar, and fun. I feel at ease and nervous around you at the same time... not wanting to trip over myself to get closer to you. You only seem to let me in a little.

I need to assure you that what I feel for you is not superficial or strictly physical. I fell for you right away, wanting to know more, wanting to share space with you, wanting to be your safe and soft landing. Your energy was electric, magnetic, melanated, magical, mystical, hypnotic! I haven't felt like that since 2008, when someone stole my cool. I can't be chill about the fire you re-ignited in me. I want to be familiar with the deepest recesses of your mind and learn your fantasies and desires.

Spending time with you has me elated and unable to contain it. Although you smile and hug me when I arrive, I often leave wondering how you *really* feel. Wondering if you feel anything... Do I make you feel good, wanted, listened to, supported, loved, or desired? Do I make you happy?

Can we talk about it? Are you able to tell me? Tell me how I make you feel, what goes through your mind when you look at me, what sensation takes over you when I touch you, kiss you...

The way you smack my ass if cross in front of you through a room, or bend over to pick something up, or while I'm cooking us dinner; perplexes me. Not heard you say much about us, but physically, you *are* expressive. The casual way you say, "You deserve it" after we make fire feels patronizing, like you pity me in some way. But I am choosing to give you my body because you stir something in me that feels good, sexy, and familiar, not for validation. It's because I want you… cosmically, physically, energetically, spiritually, and completely.

I often think about us… Simply sharing space. You shirtless and shea buttered, helping me cook. Me barefoot, donning only your tee-shirt, moving around the kitchen in a dance of flirtation. Tickling, teasing, talking shit, tasting sauces, juices; laughing, kissing, moaning, fingers slipping into wet places, hands gripping solid power. Can't always make it to bed, so you take me right where we are. Guiding my response to you with your hands. Gripping my hips, kissing my neck, whispering in my ear, breathing heavily; it slides in so nice… I grip the back of your neck, pulling you closer, licking and nibbling your earlobe, kissing your mouth slowly, deeply, teasing your tongue with mine, moving in sync with your rhythm. "A slow clap turned to rapid applause!"

Alas, another fantasy I can't openly share with you. Why are you so closed off to me? It has been 3 years of late nights, early mornings, random afternoons, and many walks on the lakefront. Why can't we talk about it…?

I don't mean to sound…. irrational; truly can't get you out of my system; I stay busy, work out, pray, and create in attempts to keep the thought of you from taking over my mind. I know these feelings are not entirely reciprocal, if at all. Just know, "I want you. In no uncertain terms, I want you."

I love you.

Yours. Always.
"Rubes"

Spoken from my heart! II

Heart, body, soul, cooking skills, sex appeal, modesty, and everything else they claim to want in a real woman...

Independence and compassion, then when they get it, act like it doesn't even matter?

And, oh, can they make you feel so idiotic for wanting to be intimate or affectionate toward them! They're at you like, "No, this ain't that! "What are you doing?" "I don't get down like that!" "Kissing is for simps. " And my all-time favorite... "You doing too much!"

But turn the tables, and *they're* aroused; it **HAS** to be every nasty, freaky, domesticated thing they want, or else there's nothing; mean jokes at your expense, strange looks, and the classic "Nah, I'm straight, I'll call you."

The question often posed is, "What do women want?!"

I found that the answer is quite simple; we want a man who is decisive, passionate, empathetic, thoughtful, a leader but not controlling, expressive, open to new ideas, creative, and kind, and above all... himself.

My question is, what are men actually in it for?

THE SITUATION-SHIP
"ARE YOU FOR REAL?"

A MINUTE AGO, WE WAS COOL...

A Kiss As Smooth As Toffee *(2006)*

You look deep within me, searching...

I return the favor, finding...

A kiss as smooth as toffee.

Slowly, we inch closer, you thinking to yourself, "How interesting it is to know her!"

Kiss as smooth as toffee.

Your fingertips caress the small of my back, mine stroking the nape of your neck, both pulling each other closer...

Kiss as smooth as toffee.

Deeper and stronger the passion grows. Every time he moves, it makes me wiggle my toes.

Kiss as smooth as toffee.

His tongue strokes mine, and I feel high. It's like the Nile is running 'tween my thighs.

Kiss as smooth as toffee.

I feel his wet, thick lips pressing as his nimble fingers slowly slip off my dress.

Kiss as smooth as toffee.

Passion and heat rise within us, my body yearning to feel his thrust!

Kiss as smooth as toffee.

And like the waiting bubbles in a champagne bottle, finally…

A kiss as smooth as toffee!

A Letter

Hey Baby,

Downloading music today, and so many of the songs reminded me of you. I made you a playlist so you can enjoy it with me. I hope they put you in the mood the way they do me!

I miss you, babe. I want to spend a day naked with you. Just naked. Walking around the house, watching TV, cooking together, dancing, we don't have to do anything we don't want to do!

I just love your naked body and how soft your skin is, how good that soft skin feels pressed up against mine. I want to lay you down, drizzle honey and chocolate, and enjoy every delicious moment that follows.

There is no one else I crave being naked with but you.

Naked with you is so much more than the physical; I feel safe, vulnerable, and open with you. I love you, Babe, now, in the past, and well into our future.

Write back soon.

Always,

"Spectacular, Spectacular"

Next Lifetime *(2007)*

Difficult Timing
Constant smiling
Can't be selfish; learning to share
No expectations, no emotions involved
Only clumsy tumbles in the dark
I guess I'll be yours next lifetime

So much laughter between us
My feelings are dripping from my lips
Like honey on hot biscuits
I guess I'll be yours next lifetime

Someone has your heart, and you can't let go
I understand now… but you say I'm "special"
I guess I'll be yours next lifetime
Hope for the best; expect the worst
I hope another girl doesn't get your heart first
If I'm the beat, then you're the rhythm
Your precious mind, like a prism
Lying with you, wishing you could hear my heart
Being that close to you somehow is still not close enough
I guess I'll be yours next lifetime

Head spinning out of control
Wish I could quiet the loud, sweet nothings floating around my mind
Can't say "no" when you call my name or reach for me in the dark
But when the light comes, I'm invisible to you…
I guess I'll be yours next lifetime.

"Of Course"

"Do you miss me?"

"Of course!"

You say that like I should know. But I didn't get your call.

Months passed, and I did not hear from you, not a "Hey baby" or "How's it going?" Or a "Can I see you?", or, my favorite... "I miss you."

"Do you think I'm pretty?"

"Of course!"

You toss it out like I should know. But you never affirm it. Yeah, you hit me with "yo' sexy ass!" while you're deep up in it, though I need to hear it while we're vertical doing absolutely nothing...

Of course, I wonder how you feel when you don't communicate much.

Of course, I have questions about "us" when we converse about everything but.

Of course, I know we are *"not serious"*, as you say. You told me you're not ready. But can't we be real friends?

Of course, I love you, *and* I can keep my emotions in check. I know how not to fall in love. How not to get my hopes up and let my imagination run away... *again.*

Of course, I have patience and can wait for God's plan to unfold in His timing. To be faithful and quiet, love myself deeply, and remember to pray.

Of course, I pray for you. Not for anything to change in you or between us, but to send you love, light, and self-awareness.

Of course, I want to share space with you. As I said, you are amazing, smart, funny, silly, interesting, and knowledgeable. A real King!

Of course, I prioritize me and mine. I make time for you because I want to, I am able to, and I enjoy doing so. No obligation, just unconditional joy.

Of course, *I* want *you* in my life.

"Can't imagine it without you," you said. At least we seem to agree on that...

"See you sooner than later?"

"Of course."

You say with such light-hearted joy. And I know it's true, but probably up to me to initiate... *again.*

Of course!

"This Water"

"My favorite water made flesh..."

Drinking, bathing, cooking. Water, ever flowing through all I do. Coconut, lemon, cucumber, and alkaline- ever hydrating me in different flavors.

But water flows in many different ways... much like our energies and spirit flow.

Family and friends carry a sediment of sentiment. Love flows freely between us, the water from ancestral lines through our blood. Once joined with each other, the crash of hugs, tears, and laughter upon our bodies and ears like waves crashing over rocks. Loud, full, and unapologetic. The water of unconditional love.

Music, rhythms, lyrics, drums, all flowing through the speaker of life, filling the silent space like water fills a jar. Full, fun, loud, prophetic, and truthful. Leaving space for joy and sorrow. Like Mamman used to tell me, "laugh and cry, Cheri, at the same time." Salty water from the eyes flows, heavy, thick, and freely. The water of true emotion.

Falling in love is comparable to your first trip down the biggest water slide at the water park. With the anticipation of what's to come, you climb to the top of the steps. Smelling the water as you edge closer to the "ride". The unspoken commitment you made to yourself to "just do it", to follow through and take the leap. Finally, it's time to let go, and you scream with excitement! The water under you propels you forward, unyielding and cold, but feels good on your sun-drenched skin. Now, the love gets more intense as you start to hit the curves, dips, twists, and turns. Picking up speed as you near the end of the ride, energy reciprocated as the force continued to grow. Suddenly, the light hits your face with the promise of a deep plunge, and depending on how you land, the outcome can be refreshing and fun or overwhelming and scary. The water of unpredictability.

Dabbling in and exploring the art of *making* water can be an adventure in pleasure. Viscous and thick water runs between my thighs as he wraps his arms around me. Wetting each other's lips with eager tongues. Fingers exploring curves and crevasses, slipping, sliding, stroking, entering. Splashing in my gentle essence, his movements flow between passionate, high-tempo strokes and slow, intentional waves, generating a flood of pleasure and desire. Paces quickened until I need a drink, asking you if you need to hydrate as well. Your reply blows my mind: "No baby, I'm focused on *this* water!" Exactly what I needed to hear. Sexual waters to quench my mind.

Still Enjoying My Yard Today...

The door swings open, and a friendly, inviting semi-familiar face smiles from ear to ear. The summer air that night was soothing. My classmate invited me over for a game of Halo 2 and a session of the sticky with his homeboys. Our host's face becomes clear as I see that it is Jerrod, a fellow Scorpio and unbeknownst to me, a future bad idea that makes a great story! As the swirls of herb smoke and peach white owls fill the room, we undress each other with our eyes, making plans without uttering a word... what a summer.

Spoken from My Heart III

Tired, fed up, resigned, irritated, heartbroken, reeling... So many attempts at being charming, sexy, or vulnerable, only to continually be rejected or run away from. I'm pissed! Mad cuz I let these fools touch my sacred spaces, mad cuz I believed their lies, mad at **myself**! Screaming into the night, *again*, will I ever fucking learn?

THE CAPTAIN OF MY SHIP

"WE HAVE A HEADING!"

"WITHOUT THE SOUR, THE SWEET AIN'T AS SWEET"...

Missing You

I know I was the one to walk away, to get fed up and say, " I'm done!"

The one who gave unconditionally and relentlessly without requiring reciprocation.

But when I close my eyes, I see your face smiling at me. I remember how buttery soft your skin was, how sexy your voice sounded when you whispered in my ear.

I wake up again, not wrapped in your arms, not wearing your T-shirt, and remember what I texted you… "You broke my heart."

I know I was the one to get fed up, walk away, and say, "I'm done!"

Certain places in the city remind me of you, of us. Songs play in the background of life, and I'm reminded of steamy nights we spent together.

I also found anger when I thought of you. You pushing me away and acting like I didn't mean anything to you…

That hurt…

In retrospect, maybe it was on purpose. Making me mad so I wouldn't hurt, but it hurt to be mad at you.

I used that energy, that anger, to put you away in a safe place, untouched. But after a while, I needed you around again, so I picked up the phone when you called.

I know I was the one to walk away, to get fed up, and say, "I'm done."

Hopeful, optimistic, in denial; thinking *'this time we'll be different.'*

At first, it *did* feel new, fresh, more real. Then, in a few short weeks, someone hit the replay button, and I started to remember.

Missing you was "like a drug that I wanted too much of." I wanted something from you that you weren't equipped to give.

My mistake was not listening to your not-so-subtle hints of unavailability, how easy it was for you to make me an option when you were my priority.

The way you resisted my love language, not letting me cook for you, saying, "you're doing too much," or accusing me of being "too nice." Making me feel stupid for loving you…

So, as much as I'm missing you, and as much as it hurts…

I got fed up, walked away, and was the one who said, "I'm done."

July 4, 2023

I am insecure

I don't trust that people truly want me

I procrastinate

I am afraid of failure

I am afraid of rejection

I am afraid of success

I am afraid of being a disappointment

I am afraid of being disappointed… again

I am afraid I am not attractive

I am worried that my trauma taints me

I am worried that I believe that I won't find reciprocal love

I need constant validation, reassurance

I often give the benefit of the doubt when I should believe the initial presentation of energy

I often let my depression win

I really can't take constructive criticism

I am defensive for no reason

I don't like being told to do something I am on my way to do

I am attracted to unavailable men

I don't like the way I look

I worry about being a good parent

I don't believe there's someone special "just for me"

I cry about everything

I need to recover my follow-through/ up

I am too generous to under-deserving energies

I have lost faith in my power

I need to get back in the practice of practice…

And these qualities make me courageous, lovable, and completely beautiful, as my perfectly imperfect human self.

I am unconditionally loved.

August 29, 2023

Remembering my flow, my power, my prowess, and my intention.

Waking each morning purposefully with much grace

Loving Ruby so deeply that the hurt starts to melt away. Showing myself that I can show up for myself… Healing.

Theme songs like "True Love" by Whiz Kid, "Free Mind" by Tems, and "Bloody Samaritan" feat. Kelly Rowland.

Sankofa- going back to get me! Remembering the sweet, simple things that make me smile from my heart… it doesn't take much to do so.

Good food, great music, my own company… real joy!

A Haiku

Hibiscus, you are…

The sweet flower of my home,

Pink, bright love at night.

Shade Me

Dear Mother, Creator,

Shade me. Shade me from the blinding light of judgment that I cast on myself. The harshness of not feeling adequate in this crazy world.

I want to love myself like You love me. Want to see how amazing I am, the way You intended.

Love You, thank you...

Your Child

Dance=Freedom

Drums, bells, tambourines, feathers, silks, shoulders, hands, fingers, eyes, earrings, jewels, anklets, scarves, moccasins, fringes, coins, beads, hips, knees, feet, toes, tradition, teaching, living...

What Does Self-Love Mean... To Me?

When I think of self-love, the cliched, stereotypical images and concepts come to mind initially. For example, bubble baths, mani-pedis, facials, and any deep cleaning hygiene practices. There are also the health and wellness concepts, like working out and eating right, taking your vitamins, etc.

However, in efforts to restart those practices in my life, I have come to realize that it involves so much more than just those seemingly pedestrian habits. It is carving out the space in my heart that it was always meant for.

Self, that I used to feed when I was younger. Chasing dreams, fantasies, and hobbies. Doing what I loved unapologetically. Spending time in nature, writing, reading, drawing, just being still. Self-love is work, a labor of love that yields the tastiest fruits. To me, it means a return, a return to better behaviors, practices, habits, and ways of speaking. A return to being kind and graceful with myself, making a small effort every day to show myself unconditional love.

To choose not to chase, to choose to lie in wait and only emerge when I have cleaned and healed my wounds, stored enough thought and love to last a dozen seasons and more. Self-love is trusting in the Divine, to send me the messages I am meant to see and for me to follow them. Trusting that the Divine has a design just for me and will walk with me as I traverse the journey that lies ahead of me. Self-love is making a promise to your higher self and keeping it. Whatever that looks like... Do it.

Ase, Ase, Ase O!

Ask Any Butterfly

Ask any butterfly, if it was easy... if it felt good?

They'd probably say, "Hell no! Change is hard!

Eating from branch to branch, trying not to get picked off by birds and squirrels.

Sleeping enough to grow another millimeter. Staying low and out of sight.

Using God given defense systems to stink bomb predators or nay-sayers.

Finding shelter under the right leaf to stay dry in the downpour.

Remembering I still have a long way to go.

Eating even more so now I'm fat and juicy... an even bigger target.

Eyes all over me judging me, sizing me, plotting their next move. Waiting for my highest point of vulnerability... ready to strike.

Reaching my pentacle, my fullest point. Time to search for the perfect perch to rest and form my cocoon.

Dragging all this weight up, and up, and up, and under the right leaf to wrap myself.

This shit is uncomfortable!"

Ask any butterfly, is it better in your cocoon?

They'd definitely say, "Hell no! This shit is scary!

Okay, now carefully weave your tail inside, while all the while looking out for hungry mouths.

Moving slowly up the body, mindfully putting myself away for what's next.

Almost there now… one final check to see that I'm still in a safe place.

Now the work really begins…

Completely exposed and unavailable.

The inevitable shift taking place, from struggle to grace, is real.

I feel it all. The pain of my body changing, the confusion of shedding old habits for new practices.

Limbs stretching, body lengthening, eyes opening, heart and mind strengthening.

This dull ache at my back, remembering everything that I went through to get here. Wings are forming through their scars from angry birds attempting to devour me.

I love my scars, they remind me how thick my skin is… my wings are gonna be so dope!"

Ask any butterfly, was it worth it?

She will pause a moment and reflect… She will flutter her wings, looking at them with deep admiration, and breathe deeply before whispering…

"Absolutely!"

LESSONS LEARNED

BORROWED QUOTES AND IMAGES

"A slow clap turned to rapid applause!"- Honey Pot Performance, Ladies Ring Shout 2.0, June 2023

"I want you. In no uncertain terms, I want you." - Stranger Than Fiction, 2006 Film

"Without the sour, the sweet ain't as sweet." - Vanilla Sky, 2001 Film

"My favorite water made flesh..." - Honey Pot Performance, Ladies Ring Shout 2.0, June 2023

www.ingramcontent.com/pod-product-compliance
Lightning Source LLC
Chambersburg PA
CBHW032214040426
42449CB00005B/589